If I Go Missing

Poems by Octavio Quintanilla

Slough Press   Kyle ~ Alamo

Copyright © 2014
All rights reserved

For orders and information:
Slough Press
334 Spring Dr.
Kyle, Texas 78640.
or
Slough Press
939 W. De Soto Ave.
Alamo, TX 78516

Cover Art by Adam Turl
Book Design by Christopher Carmona

Library of Congress Cataloging-in-Publication Data

Quintanilla, Octavio.
 [Poems. Selections]
 If I go missing : poems / by Octavio Quintanilla.
    pages cm
 Includes bibliographical references and index.
 ISBN 978-0-941720-35-9 (alk. paper)
 I. Title.
 PS3617.U5897A6 2014
 811'.6--dc23
                    2014012818

Acknowledgements

Grateful acknowledgement goes to the editors of the volumes in which these poems, some in earlier versions, first appeared:

"Landscape with a Dead Goat," & "Sonnet for Human Smugglers," *Alaska Quarterly Review*
"Mal de Ojo," "Finding My Way," *Salamander*
"Tell Them Love Is Found," RHINO
"Death Study," "Go Hungry," *South Dakota Review*
"[Those young, handsome faces]," *The Texas Observer*
"Carcass, South Texas Dirt Road," *Los Angeles Review*
"Black Throated Sparrow," *New Mexico Poetry Review*
"[My parents can't recognize the country of their birth]," *San Antonio Express-News*
"Fugitive," *American Poetry Journal*
"Agua, Name for Water,"*BorderSenses*
"If I Go Missing," *Conium Review*
"Begging," *Border Crossing*
"A Man and His Dogs," *Naugatuck Literary Review*
"Love Song with Exiles" *The Bitter Oleander*
"The Poor," "Motorcyclist, No Helmet," *Margie*
"Sonnet with All Its Grief Cut Out," "Welfare," *Eclipse*
"Landlords," *Dos Passos Review*
"In Spite of Love," *Bravado*
"Café Triste," *Anemone Sidecar*
"Strange Beds," *Spillway*
"The Sleepwalker Never Wakes Up," "Night Music," *Off the Coast*
"Thieves," *Diner*
"After Our Mothers Die," *Saltwater Quarterly*
"Home," *Thin Air Magazine*
"Sonnet for Human Smuggler," "Tough Guy," *New Border Voices: An Anthology*.
"Corpse Fauna," *Midway Journal*
"[Through plaster walls I hear the wailing]," "[You take a stranger's life]," "[Don't go hungry for my dark skin]," "[Early morning, the moon]," *Strike Magazine*
"Influx" and "Ciudad Juárez," *J Journal*

Contents

If....

The Left Hand	8
Dream Transient	10
[You take a stranger's life]	11
[A bar fight once in a while is a healthy sign]	12
Tough Guy	13
Thieves	14
Black Throated Sparrow	15
[I carry my destiny like a corpse]	16
Motorcyclist, No Helmet	17
Finding My Way	18
[The girl at the coffee house is beautiful]	19
Carcass, South Texas Dirt Road	20
Matanza del Marrano	21
Begging	23
What's To Know	24
After Our Mother's Die	25
Agua, Name for Water	26
Legacy	28
Night Visitors	29
A Man and His Dogs	30

...I Go...

[My parents can't recognize the country of their birth]	32
Love Song with Exiles	33
Sonnet for Human Smugglers	35
[Those young, handsome faces]	36
[Early morning, the moon]	37
Influx	38
Ciudad Juárez	39
Secuestro Express	40
Mal de Ojo	41
[Let's play a game]	42
[Through plaster walls I hear the wailing]	43
[The hardest thing for anyone to endure]	44
Overcoat for the Wind	45
Corpse Fauna, Frontera	46
Promise	47
Night Music	48

The Poor	49
[Don't go hungry for my dark skin]	51
Death Study	52
The Helpless and the Lost	53
Welfare	54

...Missing

Parents	56
Sleepwalker Never Wakes Up	57
[I keep returning to the days]	58
Strange Beds	59
Tell Them Love Is Found	60
Why We Can't Marry	61
All There Is	62
The Game	64
Pretending	65
Café Triste	66
Landscape with Dead Goat	67
Go Hungry	68
Message	69
Landlords	71
Ramona, Mostly Naked, Mostly Sane	72
Drawing Humans and Animals, Heads Represented by Circles, Bodies by Straight Lines	73
Fugitive	75
Birth	76
Heaven	77
Sonnet with All Its Grief Cut Out	79
Box of Pennies	80
[All of us have a story]	81
If I Go Missing	82

"Sé que hay una persona
que me busca en su mano, día y noche,
encontrándome, a cada minuto, en su calzado"—

    César Vallejo, "Poema Para Ser Leído Y Cantado"

"I know there is a person
who looks for me in her hand, day and night,
finding me, every minute, in her shoes"—

    César Vallejo, "Poem To Be Read and Sung"
        (trans. by Clayton Eshleman)

If...

"Órdenes al corazón: lamer el rocío de la bendición de los ausentes"-

-María Baranda

"Orders to the heart: lick the dew of the blessing of the absent"
(trans. by Monica de la Torre)

The Left Hand
After Carlos Drummond de Andrade & Mark Strand

I'm tired of having the same dream
every night, I said,
the dream in which I lose my left hand
doing a job I wasn't born to do.
Sometimes I'm picking trash
on the side of the highway.
Other times, I'm saving a drowning man.
Sometimes it's an electric saw
that jags my hand off.
Last night, it got chopped clean
by a butcher's knife, weird
because as a boy I admired butchers
and liked their knives.
Brown and soft, my left hand
bloodies the floor.
This hand that has done the slapping
and the punching gets punished
by a force that's stronger, in dreams,
than God.
It's the same hand that broke a beer bottle
on a man's head when he called me
hijo de puta.
The same one dogs nuzzle for affection.
As soon as my hand is gone,
I remember it as a gentle animal
starving for the touch
of something other than that of the right hand.
Maybe that's what it was:
The starving that turned it into an enforcer.
I'm awake now and I have no way
to tell you that even though I live with two hands
one always goes missing in my dreams.
What does that say about my life?
If I ever dream my hand floating down a river,

should I follow it?
Where would it take me?
The salmon and the catfish will know
I'm crazy. Look at this fool, they'll say,
and laugh the laugh that only they can hear.
They've waited centuries for me
to dip my feet into the water.
They knew I would come and try
to take what no longer wants
to be a part of me.
Just so you know,
I always have enough time
to step out of the river
and make my way home.
I find you packing your bags,
closing the curtains, locking the door.
You can't see me but I see you,
and the night returns, and so does the river,
and the hand that rides the current
to the ocean
and refuses to drown.

Dream Transient
After reading Roberto Bolaño

I'm in one of Borges' dreams. He chases me like a dog. I try to dream of the word *labyrinth*. Borges doesn't let me. He tells me it's impossible to give it shape. In his dream I'm not allowed to dream. He said.

I dream I see through my grandfather's eyes. I see a man folding dollar bills into his wallet. I see a paper gun. I see the shawl of a woman, and a woman without a shawl. I see grief as spider. I see bottles of beer. I see a man falling off a horse. I see a cactus. I see. He was blind.

My daughter tells me she had a dream about me. I sketched a house made of cardboard. Then I preached inside the house. Then there was a mob. Someone ran me out of town. I found a river. I crossed the river. I found a woman. The woman was her mother. I loved her mother. Then I woke up. I told my daughter I had a dream about her.

I dream my ex-lover dreams about me. We hold hands. We kiss. We have a black child. He calls me by another man's name. His mother tells me I'm worthless. She makes the child disappear. We're alone. My hands and feet are tied. She whips me with the wet backbone of adultery. I try to remember her name so she may stop. Andrea. Samantha. Mercy.

[You take a stranger's life]

You take a stranger's life
And hide it under your shirt.
You take it home and make sure
The neighbors don't see it.
You smuggle it past your mother
Who's in the kitchen pouring water
Into a pot of beans.

This life you've taken fits
Under your mattress.
It bawls like an orphaned pup
And you hush it
With promises to release it.
But you won't.

You've always thought
It was a good idea
To have a life to spare,
Like the spare tire in your trunk,
Just in case someone came along
And took yours.

[A bar fight once in a while is a healthy sign]

A bar fight once in a while is a healthy sign
you still want to live.

God's good purpose sits
at the bottom of the drink
you have every morning
to prove you're man.

Once, someone told you:
Eres chingón.
Eres macho.

The trees ignore you
because you're not a tree.
People ignore you
because you're not a tree.

Still, you want to talk to them,
let them know
you want to start over.
You want to find a new opponent
more dangerous than the universe.

This is the way to go because
eres un macho chingón.

You need it now,
before the mirror forgets
what you look like,
before water forgets
how to drown you.

Tough Guy

My brother points with the red nipple
of a cigarette to a guy sporting
trendy jeans and flip flops.
"Pussy," he says.
"If you open him up,
you'd see he has no guts."

When drunk, he pours milk
between the legs of a beautiful girl,
and licks.
Then he returns to a time
when the sound of his name
pushed him to the end of the lunch line.

Hardly anyone could pronounce it.
Teachers tried to rename him.

Years later, he wants to go back.
He is still crouching under
the gym bleachers, trembling
at the principal's office.
The boy in this bar forgets
he no longer has anything
to prove.

But prison breastfed him scorpions.
Now when he goes out,
he carries our mother's prayer
like a necklace.

On his chest, the suffering
face of Christ,
     bloody nest for birds.

Thieves

Who cares about who gets caught
jumping over someone else's fence?
Mutts will bark.
Porch lights will sweep small critters
into another darkness.
Big deal.
Nothing will be stolen.
They came to lie on your bed.
Slip on your sandals.
Touch your daughter's drawings.
But know that some of them need
to get caught
and so will leave you
fingerprints sealed in plastic bags.
You'll find them on the table,
next to the green apples and the crumbs
of grief you leave for the hungry
wind to take.
Some will return the next day
and wait for you,
will sit on the doorstep,
apologize.
I'm sorry, one will say, but I live a sad life.

Black Throated Sparrow

Life's oil;
  to clean it, I need
the finger that condemns me

and the hands that set on fire
  all the fools who believe
in mercy.

Crucified, Christ suffers
  on a man's forearm;
always homeless,

He makes His presence known
to the forlorn chosen
for sacrifice.

His wing is the whore
with a dream.
His dagger, the young thug
sobbing in a city jail.

Leave Christ in His nest,
and glide over fools
  who transmit sunlight
with a touch;

Point to the men
  outlived by their children
and to the children outlived
by their desires.

My eye inside yours
  looks past me
to cross histories
that have no place for us.

Out there, you lord over fields.

[I carry my destiny like a corpse]

I carry my destiny like a corpse
of someone I've known
all my life.
A faithful pet.
A true enemy.
Heavy like a bad deed
I have not yet committed.

Today I have no words,
no silence, no images to release
like frightened birds
out of their cages.

I think of the word "forgiveness"
and I can't force it to forgive.
Can't say, "Forgiveness is like…"
No simile.
No metaphor.
Just talk.

If you find beauty in this,
then you know the human heart
is made of words.

Motorcyclist, No Helmet

Because you see a skull in the belly
    of a leaf. Because the earth wants
        your return. Because everything calls you
            by the name your parents didn't give you.
                Because the bed traps you
                    as you leave behind the footprints
              of your failure. What you have never been
remembers you.
                    You backpack fear. You fear
            to breathe. You leave this night
    because waiting for eternity takes too long.
    Now the wind is a woman who smokes.
  Because it's late. Because no one will track you
and end your misery.

Finding My Way

I want to find the way of ants,
how they build dirt mounds
out of human flesh,
how they destroy and then carry
the little corpses
of leaves and twigs
on their tiny backs.
I want to find my way into their fetching
a brittle strand of hair
from a tree branch
where a young bride
left a promise to the moon.
There's a way into all things,
into a strand of hair, for instance,
or into the DNA of a star.
I want to find the way of ants
that crumple my skin like a piece
of white paper—
a way into all things,
into the eye broken into
by the crowbar of light,
making a mess of what we see,
making a mess out of truth.

[The girl at the coffeehouse is beautiful]

The girl at the coffeehouse is beautiful.
She reads a book and I wonder
if the male character who talks to her
is handsome.
I wonder, *Is she listening to the footsteps of a woman*
who's burdened by a guilty conscience?
Maybe her guilt has to do with her lawn,
big as a cemetery.
Or her bathroom, clean
as a baby's nails.
Where has the traffic gone?
Outside, in the summer heat,
an old man starts a fire
to warm what's left
of his dignity.
He's one of many who've lost the papers
that'd prove they are who they say they are.
I want to read about how our ailing mattresses
will not carry our bodies
for much longer,
how our eyes will never be deep enough
to store the light that keeps abandoning us.
Who will read to us?
Who would want to read us?
God can't save us all.

Carcass, South Texas Dirt Road

You still remember how it looked
        after the drizzle licked it clean.

What the hell was it?

        Blades of grass
    taking the place of teeth;
    the wind's snout
        sniffing sockets for a light
    long gone.

You must've been nine years old,
    old enough to know that dust is raised
to fall on dust again.
Old enough to keep secrets.

Years turned horror into poetry.

Maybe you want to go back.
    To the wood-framed house sitting
    on concrete blocks.
        To the mutt you saved from drowning
    in a canal. To the girl
    who had no faith in you.

She had a pretty yard.
Her father worked for the city.
Maybe you don't want to remember her.

Or that your father was without legal papers.
        All day digging trenches
    for plumbers, always walking
    on the dusty colonia road
    that darkened when wet

like a monument for old bones.

Matanza del Marrano

Winter, to celebrate the birth
of Jesus, my brothers buy a pig,
sometimes a goat,
and sacrifice it in the name
of good times. The youngest one,
who has a love affair with guns,
shoots it in the forehead, and the pig
often too large to be disheartened
by the bullet, takes a step back
and charges forward to welcome
the second shot.
Now the boys stretch it on a table
and their knives begin to cut
into fatty tissue, pulling at the flesh
and at the coarse hair that peels
as easy as a shirt.
After the skinning is done,
my brothers,
and friends who came to watch and talk,
stand around the animal
and smoke cigarettes as they wipe their knives
along the sides of their legs.
They're young as they stand here,
trying to reclaim a ritual
they could've lost
the day their father left his country
to give them a new one.
Their knives learn to open flesh
as their eyes keep watch for what's hidden
in the belly's chamber.
They keep finding the root
that refuses to be cut.
Maybe their sons, too, one day,
will learn to use a knife to see,
to feel they belong somewhere.

For now, someone will say
a joke in Spanish,
and someone will repeat
parts of it in English,
and laughter will scatter along the fields
like a flock of hungry wrens.

Begging

I was young once, and once I jumped into a body
Of water where a body I did not know

Stared back into the sun's red pupil.
Its permanent gaze sick with absence,

No light, no dark, one hundred and fifty pounds
Slowly floating like unwanted jetsam,

Dissolving down the stream
Like the afterimage of a ship made flesh

On its way to a city I had no name for.
It must've roamed with the current

Many days and nights, a knife-wound, I imagined,
Or someone's final plunge to release the world.

And how to get it back, I wonder, still,
After all these years. I told my mother about the body,

And about my body and she warned me not to show
the softness that trembled underneath my clothes.

Let it be, she said, and you'll learn the whiteness
Of a fire and the clamor of the burned,

The slow ebb of what you've known.
To never ask for its return.

What's To Know

I laughed when the kid said, I is your friend,
But didn't know he'd been kidding till much later,
Later when I found out he'd been shot
By a stray bullet, a bullet so old it was impossible
For it to allow him to keep on living.
This living satisfies no one,
Not even the silly gods that fear us,
That keep making errors
And yet keep trying, keep taking off
Their clothes and pointing a gun
At everything, save their temples, that needs
an ounce of light.
Yet still I believe I'm thicker than water,
Sweeter than blood,
Saner than whiskey,
And all this laughter, all this foolery,
Has something to do with grief.

After Our Mothers Die

So easy to believe in nothing,
To believe in God,
                        To believe we are not

Tired of the taste the worms leave
In the hook of our mouth.

So easy to slam the door *goodbye*,
                   forget you, screw you,
To arrive at the place

Where no one waits with a kind word,
A cup of soup, a key to unlock
                   Whatever keeps us locked.

So easy to curse the meal we eat
Alone after a long journey,
                   To curse the journey,

                   And enter a house
Where our mothers
Have abandoned their infinite strength,
Their solitude, the frayed
                   Strings of their aprons.

Agua, Name for Water

Like a mad woman, the morning light passes
underneath my window,
dragging a rope with all the things that died
the night before.
If I were to get out of bed and look,
I'd see my father's angry fist
the day the white boss gave him less
than what he'd earned.
I'd see the yellow school bus and the kid
I punched in the face for making fun
of the way I pronounced water.
I'd just arrived from a country where words
sound the way they look
on a page.
If I look out the window,
I'd see Ms. Barnes asking me to read
Shakespeare in front of the class.
I thought I was a tough guy so I refused.
I wrote a poem instead.
And If I look out this window,
I'll see that poem, clinging to the skirts
of all the women who could never call me
by my true name.
They gave me nicknames that never tasted
as sweet as the name my father gave me.
Truth was, it took too much heart
to pronounce three syllables
that could not promise eternity.
This is how love works.
All the unpaid overtime.
My hand wakes on your thigh,
and now I must think about this day
that enters our lives like birth.
Though you're next to me, and I could wake you,
and I could whisper in your ear how I came

so close in my dream to drowning,
I reach for my phone and text you:
I'm the son without sons.

Legacy

*

Not in this life, but in another,
I had a woman, and the woman
had a baby.

Before breakfast,
I thought of misfortune.

Lawnmower, stolen.
Crow, white with maggots.

*

One day, cold turned
clouds into small black goats.
They wanted me
to follow them to the town
where I was born.

I licked their scent.
Licked the wool of their being.
That night I carried water
by its hips.

*

I tell my son
what my father told me:
"In your mouth this milk
will feel as warm as a hand
inside a cow's vagina."

He doesn't laugh,
but looks into me
like a deer gazing
into the eye
that will bring peace.

Night Visitors

They watched us sleep
before eating leftovers.
They smelled bread
and then pushed small fists
of it into their mouths.
They must've been starving.
They must've walked for days.

When they left, they took
our work boots and our coats.
Then, as if blessing
the earth, they scattered
gentle laughter and dragged
behind them the whimper
of the neighborhood dogs.
In the morning,
dogs refused to talk.
Their bellies disowned hunger.
Their brains looked
for their skulls.

Here, few things break
the gallop of our bodies
that bring us closer
to our first born.
If you are afraid,
close your eyes

and imagine
that cane fields are on fire,
and love, water
in our thoughts.

A Man and His Dogs

This morning
the man who died two years ago
was feeding his dogs.
He was patient and the smaller pup
came up and licked his hand.

I called out to him as you slept.
He came to my window, his dogs
followed him, wagging their tongues with joy,
rubbing their fur coats against his legs.

When you opened your eyes, I wanted
to tell you that getting lost is possibility.
Tell you, from now on if I say *sadness*
it means I am driving and I know
exactly where I am going.

I began to tell you, "Do you remember
the man who lived..." Then I stopped
when I saw you stretch your body with a yawn
as if announcing to the world
you had just been born.

...I Go...

"This is her home
    this thin edge of
        barbwire"
-Gloria Anzaldúa, *Borderlands / La Frontera*

[My parents can't recognize the country of their birth]

My parents can't recognize the country of their birth.
On the streets, children know the names of their enemies.
Grandmothers no longer close their eyes at the sound
of gunfire breaking a neighbor's window.
Towns and villages are empty.
In the cities, men and women bury the details of their lives
in coffins.
Caution is the prayer of the day.
In a bad dream at least we know beforehand who plots
against us, who trails our children on their way to school.
In a bad dream, we wake to know we're dreaming.
But here, few are lucky and many are born
with their future fixed around their neck.
My parents return to Mexico in daydream.
"One day I'll go back and wait for my grandchildren to visit
me," my mother says.
My father wants to go back and harvest the fields he worked
as a boy.
I remember those fields.
They belonged to my father and to his father and to all
the fathers who came before him.
In those fields, cows and goats grazed on sunlight
under a sky so wild, and so blue,
that it was impossible to imagine
any other existence.

Love Song with Exiles

November. The devil's keys
dangle from its neck.
The dry leaves we step on
look like small hands
missing thumb and index finger.

Men in other countries feel its dampness,
see its black stain like a shawl on chickens
scurrying to their coops.
These men have no land
and the land of others remains quiet and pale
like a face adrift in a casket.

Here, the night dies of cirrhosis.
Two months and your dogs still wait for you
as if waiting for daybreak.
Your mother brings me soup
on Sundays and fills my forehead with kisses.
Once she brought me a handful of snow
and left her pulse in the embers to keep me warm.
I'll survive, I said,
and when she said your name,
her tongue turned to foam.

In other countries, the dry cough that rises
from the hearts of women
has no choice
but to hang itself.
Through holes in the walls,
the women watch their men fold
goodbyes like pieces of paper.

The men promise to return,
but even their names will be erased

by the drizzle falling on the pavement.
Their women will never sell their babies.
Babies sucking their thumbs.
Babies so small you could carry them in purses.

Sonnet for Human Smugglers

Take care of them. If they want water,
    Dump them in the river. If they crave
Freedom, let them loose among rattlesnakes.
    If they want to breathe, let them breathe dust.

Let the desert mouse nest in their white bones.
Give them shelter with your greed. With your rape.

The road kill is a sign you're almost home.
    Point to it and show them who they are.
Their life's a documentary, a newscast.

    But for you, everything is possible.
You're the map that leads them astray,
    Priest leading a funeral procession.

Load this cargo. Shackle them with promises,
    Backaches that keep them from killing you.

[Those young, handsome faces]

Those young, handsome faces
will soon turn to leather.
Their palms, like running a finger on brick;
their eyes, spit-yellow.

When I drive past them,
their backs bent to Texas highways,
pools of sunlight on their napes,
I think of the men of my youth:
Beto, Luis, Robert, El Maistro.
I also think about my brothers
who got saved by office jobs:
air conditioning, clean white shirts, cologne.

But our father kept at it
till his body said, *No mas.*
No more to sun and dirt,
to rain and cold.
No more to steel-toe boots
and to the Texas dust that he'd soon become.
No mas to the time-card
love's drudgery
makes us keep.

[Early morning, the moon]

Early morning, the moon
On one side of the road,
The sun on the other.
I'm driving down a stretch
Of Texas highway.
The barbed wire keeps
The cows and coyotes in.
Sometimes a rabbit or a feral hog
Escapes and it's crushed
By an 18-wheeler.
The splatter reddens asphalt.
Not long ago I saw a kid
In jeans and blue cap
Climb over the fence.
I was driving fast,
About eighty mph,
And through the rear-view mirror
I saw him jump
And land on his feet.
He adjusted his cap,
And with the moon
On one side of the road
And the sun on the other,
He headed North.

Influx

Too much killing
south of the border, the heavy rains
make it easier for bodies to disappear.
    And so,
the dead come from Argentina, El Salvador, and Mexico,
as if looking for a new start.
But we know better.
    Some drift quietly to our porches or get stuck
between the branches of mesquites.
Others find their way into our cars, grin
behind the steering wheel
as if relieved to finally get home.
It's a common sight and no one bothers them.
Their foreheads have a gunshot wound or a message.
    Eventually, the water will return to where it came
and we'll see the tops of hills.
We'll see clouds, small birds, and maybe we'll even see
a small plane lose itself
in the folds of the sky.

Ciudad Juárez

As water you come into my bed
Gallop
In this blood
Dawn's soft horse
The jaw and the hoof print
The mirror and not
What it reflects
Take the rooster's angry crow
And the boy who found two
Decapitated heads
In an ice chest
A warning in the open eyes
In the bruised lips
This could happen to you
As water you came
As water you leave
Your blouse is wet with skin
Heavy with child
Swollen
Take me take us
But don't say
Breathing is just
Another way to die
That greed is the black mouth
Of the poor

Secuestro Express

If you look into your rotting molar
with a magnifying glass,
you'll see pliers and a rusty hook.
Two hands will help you find the blade
of your left shoulder and hang you.
You'll see a black mask,
two eyes peering from within
its darkness,
white teeth strong enough to bite
a piece off your face.
If you look into your rotting molar,
it'll be hard to listen
for your life's worth.
No nightmare,
but a homemade video
sets the mind on fire.
It's better to go on to work.
Go on to lunch.
To the movies.
To the butcher's.
To the hospital.
To the park.
Go on, but don't forget
on your way out
the small black comb
you always carry in your back pocket.
Take it with you.
Your mother will know it's yours.

Mal de Ojo

> "Toward evening
> When I grow bored
> I try to imagine my killer"— Novica Tadić, "Toward Evening"

The evil eye was born at the same time as light.
Let there be light,
and the good eye became full of it,
like a lung is filled by air.
All countries on earth must suffer its presence.
Its gaze has followed me
to this city,
and as I drive to work, I can't help
but think about my murderer
who is strong enough to wrestle me
to the trunk of a car
and take me on a journey
only a nightmare can devise.
If only we could see the evil hiding in the eye,
see a rat's skull shaping the pupil,
the glimmer of a sharpened ax
instead of an iris.
I wonder, as the traffic
comes to a halt,
who will notify those who wait for me
at the table of disheartenment,
who will knock at the door,
stutter my name.

[Let's play a game:]

Let's play a game:
You disobey your parents
and sneak out the window
and end up at this bar
where I've waited centuries for you.
I tell you that I like your lipstick,
your hair, your jeans that fit like skin.
You blush. You want more.
We have small talk
and share a cigarette.
I let you taste the whiskey off my lips.
You're ready, so I take you
for a drive in my pick-up
and bring you to my Room of Torture.
I scrub my body with your identity.
I peel back your hair and expose
the spoiled milk of your brain.
I suck the Judas out of you.
Nothing against you,
I swear,
but I must say,
your corpse looks much prettier
than the life you intended to live.

[Through plaster walls I hear the wailing]

Through plaster walls I hear the wailing
Of my neighbor in pain.
She casts her screams like fishing nets
Over the night's undertow.
I want to say a prayer,
But the words clog
At the root of my tongue.
Dios te salve, María...
I imagine someone is with her,
Taking her hand,
Soaking her forehead
With a wet towel.
Maybe her daughter,
Or her son,
Anyone brave enough to nudge
Her lips with drops of water.
I imagine someone enters my room
And keeps me from falling off the bed.
But someone is always falling.
Our first grief is what sets our house on fire.
By this light, we travel
Across the wire of the night.

[The hardest thing for anyone to endure]

The hardest thing for anyone to endure
must be the aging, broken body that lies upon the youth
we feel and think we still are.
I thought about my Grandfather.
How young he was when he talked about women.
He was close to ninety when he died,
and still, in his deathbed, he wanted
to hear music.
Sometimes the night emboldens us to wake the heart
that's gone deaf.
We want to fill it with sound
so the body can rise from its ashes
and begin anew.
The grackles are preaching again,
but where's the altar where I can leave
my offering?
Through the window I see a young couple.
Their faces bright with curiosity,
their moist hands reaching for each other
as if to touch for the first time.

Overcoat for the Wind
for Jesus Pérez

City where distance
is measured in smog.
Kilometers, the measure of all want.

And I thought of us, our words
made of sobs, the task of finding out
which one contained our death sentence.

No use. You were so at peace
with how much you knew about your dying
(and who wouldn't be?)
that you touched and called on all
you couldn't take. The small garden

where your veins sipped the hours.
Your mother's name written
on the palm of your hand.

Was this your way of saying *resignation*?
Or something else?

It was so long ago.
By now, not even the earth remembers
the taste of your memory.

I still find myself here
where the night is not night enough
to conceal the black dove
of your sigh.
The night's root, palpitating, calls my name,
but it's never long enough to reach
the small chamber
where the heartbeat is air.

Corpse Fauna, Frontera

1
Here, a stove is luxury.
An indoor toilet.
A cup of clean water.

2
Elsewhere, black heart
of the festering fruit.
White grin of flies.
Body hanging from a bridge.

3
Here, second hand shoes.
Horse's dry prepuce.

4
Elsewhere, dinner:
fist of hair.

5
Elsewhere, head full of lice.
Blow flies forcing the mouth to open.

Promise

I've told myself that if my brother dies
in war, say, in Afghanistan,
I'd tattoo the love I have for this world
somewhere on my body.
On my shoulder,
I would sign his name,
or on my chest,
close to the heart
that has known no grief
big enough to curse the god
that placed it there.
Under his name, then,
the Orphan Snake on Fire
I will ink into the flesh,
the Holy Mother of Machine Guns
and Suicidal Bomber wrapping its legs
across my upper back.
Further down, Saint Judas blessing
traitors and thieves
with his bony lips
and the Holy Ghost of War
hanging half-naked from a barren tree.
My new skin:
the Devil's Crooked Eye winking
at a virgin decked with the shawl of lust.
I've told myself that if my brother must die,
let him die at birth.
Or return him to his home, Lord,
and let him bear amongst friends
and cold beers whatever hell
he must bring back.

Night Music

Brother,
  where did you leave your crutches?
Where is the glass-eye given to you as a gift
in Kabul?

No more asking what is consciousness.
No more games of hide-and-seek with our mother's voice.

I know you still live
because enough coffins remain
  for those of us who wait to die.

  No more booze to soothe the crippled and the dead.
  No more fondness for spade and trowel.

Brother,
  whose knife carved a star
on your nape?
It burns into your skin,
mixes with the blaze inside of you.

No more music leaping out of windows.
No more phone calls to those who wait.

Brother,
  the song you sing can't prove
you have existed.

  No more heaven for the baptized.
  No more doorways for your empty suit to walk through.

Wait for us to bring lightning, brother,
  and fill you like a fire fills a house
when everyone is home.

The Poor

"Wer jetzt kein Haus hat, baut sich keines mehr"--Rilke

At night my body climbs out
of my thoughts. Born blind,
its hands lead it to the street.
It meets the tax collector
and the priest. I say, *Good evening*,
and by that I mean, *At least you
have somewhere to go.*

Walking backwards,
I search for what the night takes
under its trees. It feeds
and then surrenders
to the streetlight and the gutter.

*Is that the moon
or a bird on fire?*

In this light, things appear to be
made more of anger
than of flesh,
like the history of all exiles
and of hands poisoned
by pesticide.
Small heartbeats
that empty their grief
all over America.
Third World countries.
Roads end where cities
keep their orphans.

Today's special news report
is about garbage scavengers.
They haul cabbage and rotting
asparagus for soup.
They want a chair, a faucet, a stove.

One of them finds an aluminum can.

A child is lucky.
He goes home empty handed.

[Don't go hungry for my dark skin]

Don't go hungry for my dark skin.
Don't go hungry for a homeland.
You ask why you must love a country
That doesn't love you back.
Isn't this the way of all love?
The nature of hunger?
You've forgotten the names of the birds
That fly above you.
You've forgotten the name of the tree
That gives you the fruit of its shade.
Your fingerprints swim like fish
In the currents of the rivers you crossed.
You want to swim after them,
Jump in the water and drift like a twig
Until you reach shore.
What shore?
The wind has erased the North Star
From the dark page of the sky.
If you could only glue together
All the torn pieces of the map
That guided you.
Follow the toll of your empty stomach.
Drink my bone marrow.
Take my hand as if taking a slice of bread.

Death Study

1
It's in the eye of strangers

                                  as you pass by.

In the movement of your hand,

                                  writing.

In the breeze,

                                  thick as fog.

2
Insatiable belly,

                                  nostril full of sand.

With each passing   day,

a little more lost

                                  in your nightgown.

3
See it for yourself:

                                  Eyes of the dying beast:

Black mirrors,   reflecting

the quick light of

                                  a falling star.

The Helpless and the Lost

Your body is a cup
of warm blood,
a spoonful of nakedness.
Give it all and I'll take it all
in mouthfuls.
So much to say,
but words have left us
alone to turn on each other
with the shard of silence.
There has to be more than this.
More than this holding
and this whiskey that squeezes
out of our skin.
More than this cage of nostalgia
that keeps me wanting more.
Take it all, but leave my obsessions behind
so they can sip the last drop of my sleep,
the last gulp of my living.
It's late, so late, after all,
that even the petty thief knows
the time has come to bless
the fruit of his labor,
the lost find a dim star in the sky,
and even those wanting
to remain anonymous,
are giving up
their names.

Welfare

As long as our stoves fatten with heat,
we bring order to our tables.
We declare to the universe:

We are masters here.

Today, winter is the old beggar
we welcome into our homes.
We let him have it all,
even the blanket we fight over
when days resemble the ribcage

some animal's flesh abandoned
by the side of the road.
One of us points to the remains.
They become symbol and fable:
Once we ate dirt moistened by rain.
Once we fed each other sleep.

Now we are going somewhere.
Let us rejoice, then, and remember the days
when our tongue was the only meat
we could bite into.

...Missing

"Out of respect for someone missing, I have to say
This isn't the whole story"
— Larry Levis, "In the City of Light"

Parents

O how they stay behind to tend
      wounds that most of us don't know.
My father licking the salt
out of my mother's grief.
My mother putting a band-aid
      on my father's empty hands.

Their voices get quieter by the day, like music
      that slowly freezes in the air.
Their bodies, bars of soap
stranded in water.

      On mild afternoons they stroll parks,
laugh for what they miss.
Then they return
      to the house where we left all
that was useless.

What they see is not enough.
An empty coffee cup on the table.
Young faces smiling in photographs.
A baby's shoe.

      Some nights they talk about us,
            their children, who live in distant cities,
who without knowing
      also practice being alone.

Sleepwalker Never Wakes Up

My father fell from a tall ladder
at the cotton gin. I imagine, before he hit
concrete, he asked, *Where am I going?*
but in Spanish because it's the only language
that can tell him that dying is possibility. Later,

Pedro said he found him lying like a sack of potatoes,
out cold, his eyes half-way open
as if about to wake from a nap.

*

My father still wants to drive, still wants
to mow the lawn and hammer the last
nail on the unfinished cabinet.
He is here one moment, and soon after,
we see him take a walk to 1970,
when, as a young man, he helped
his grandfather, Juan, break horses,
or worked till dawn, irrigating the corn fields.

*

He worked alone, guiding water with a hoe
as he himself was gently guided by moonlight
as he is now guided by his five-year-old granddaughter
who asks, *Me compras un dulce?* and he buys her
a candy that sweetens her mouth
like her words sweeten his,
and they walk back to us, looking both ways
before crossing the street.

[I keep returning to the days]

I keep returning to the days
before I began to lose my hair,
to the days before I lost a tooth
in a bar fight,
to the nights when the love of my life
was not much older,
maybe a year or two,
than my oldest daughter.
I'm not lost.
I'm here, a bystander at the margins
of this great universe
where there is no such thing as miracles.
Mary never had an Immaculate Conception.
Jesus never rose from the dead.
Those who sleep well at night
have never had their wrists
slit by worry.
The rest of us: potential suicides.
Let's face it:
It's hard to keep a straight face
once our disappointment puts on a gray coat,
a black hat, and drives around the city
looking for God, wanting to know the truth.
Documents get burned every day.
Many are falsified.
Things that evoke memory also get lost.
Some are left behind at bus stations
or at parks where people set themselves
on fire with loneliness.
But there must be a star in this great galaxy
that knows the true place and time of my birth.
I'm driving again.
Lit by the car's headlights,
the road seems to go on forever.

Strange Beds

Having never known

they unclip hairpins

of panties.

where a light unknown

guides them

of one man

How they want

that explains

everything to do

How they want

can recognize,

"I'm here,"

like forgiveness,

that quiets

their fathers,

and slip out

They climb beds

to the rest of us

from the arms

to those of another.

a gesture

failure has nothing,

with love.

a touch their memory

a voice that says,

a gentle voice

morsel of tenderness

all beckoning.

Tell Them Love Is Found

Tell your mother all about us, and tell
Your brothers too, the two who hate me
And the one who takes your lipstick
From your purse when he thinks no one watches.
I see him touching his face in the black coffee,
Staring into his own eyes like a lover into those of the beloved.
He loves himself. So what?
He will love a man. So what?
No one needs to know about him,
Not your brothers, not your father, not your mother
Who disappears a little more each day
Into dirty pans, into orange flame
That rises from the stove
After all forgiveness is wiped clean.
But tell her about us.
Tell her to tell your father
And to tell your brother who's in love with me
And the other two who want to cut my eyes out
With a piece of broken mirror.
Assemble all of them like pieces of a puzzle,
Even if you no longer know what it is
You're assembling,
And tell them.
Tell them that I'll keep returning to this house
And gently take what is no longer theirs.
Tell them I'm afraid
That they'll never miss us.

Why We Can't Marry

On a wet napkin you draw a fly
inside a horse's eye.
You say this is all
your childhood left you,
the only thing that never passes on
and remains to hold you
like an urn.
Empty-handed you arrive,
no coins to jingle in the pockets
of your coat, no inheritance,
not even a kiss that'd give hope
to whoever sees its print
on your forehead.
You bring nothing but a toothbrush
and yet you ask
for coffee, detergent, wedding vows.
I have no answers but a shrug
to say I'm homeless.
Leave your mother where she lies.
She's exhausted from going
here to there.
Tell her to turn on the radio,
to watch TV,
to sit somewhere and rest
so the world can begin to make
a living out of her.
There's not much we can do,
even now as we stumble on each other
looking for a way
out of these endless nights,
an exit that'll takes us
to another destination no mind
in its right mind
would conceive.

All There Is

The last time I got wasted was the night
I lost my wedding ring.
God knows where I left it,
or who took it.
If I could remember maybe
I'd realize I flipped it out the window
as I drove home from the bed
of a one-night stand.
But I don't remember.
I pawned it for gas, I said,
and for the first time I saw a wrinkle
on your face.
I'd hated wrinkles my whole life.
It was hard to look at loved ones in the eye.
I always saw my old leather shoes.
My father's belt.

I wondered if you wanted
to keep going, if you'd keep the promise
you made one crazy drunken night—
to wipe my ass and feed me if ever
I broke my back and couldn't move fingers
nor feet, not even twist a smile to say
thank you.
We laughed at the thought and you said,
Yes! Yes! Yes!

We've been here long enough, so long
I can't imagine not growing old
like hens poking at the dawn,
talons scratching a small mirror
where our faces remain dust.

But I still wonder if you're more than this.
More than mirror.

More than dust.
More than our twelve-year old daughter
confessing to a classmate
she's in love.
Her giggles brought you
to tears as we eavesdropped on news
not meant for us to hear.
She's old enough, I said,
and you said, *For what*?
I looked at you and smiled,
held your hand like a small human skull
and told you the truth about the night
I found you.

The Game

You bring me Jack on the rocks
and lie next to me, your skin
warm against my face, your lips
almost touching my jaw.
I'm not leaving you, I whisper as I sip
the drink, the ice cubes knocking
against my teeth.
For a second I bite the glass,
anticipating what you'll say,
wondering if it'll be the same
as other nights when all we have is words
whose power heals
only what has not been wounded.
But you don't say anything.
You rest your head on my chest
and listen to my heart
clawing its way out.
Nothing to say, I guess, after
an entire afternoon of knowing
that what has brought us here
will also lead the way
into the barren field that is not-knowing.
After I'm gone,
you'll go out with friends
and drink and be petted
by small critters your smile
manages to trap.
Who knows, you might take a liking
to one and bring him
to this bed that knows everything
about us, even the silence
that soaks us.
I'll be home, playing hide and seek
with my emotions,
dealing one more hand of poker,
and as always,
letting my wife win.

Pretending

When I kiss you, I kiss
someone else.

Sometimes it's your sister.
Other times, your mother.

Both come to me pretending they are you.

But I love the *you* I carry into bed,
half-drunk, half-asleep, breath

gasping for less of itself;
mouth, cluster
of dark blue grapes,

cluster of "I'm sorrys,"
mouth pretending
to be a mouth.

When I kiss someone else,
I kiss you.

Café Triste

Three of us and each of us
waiting for the others to leave.
The man with the hat pretending
to read the newspaper. I pretend
I am old news.

The hands of the waitress tremble
like white pigeons in the cold.
She's cut right out of *Vogue*, glossy
lips and straight, long hair
that'd close the eyelid of insomnia.

We are alone now.
The man with the hat leaves
his ulcer sitting at the table.
The waitress, not sad enough
to speak to me, pours herself
out the window.

I pretend I have what matters.
A job. A plan. Hands that come off
with the gloves.

But as always, some guy
who is wrong about the world
will come along
and make bigger claims,

and she will not remember this night,
filling and refilling a stranger's cup.

Landscape with Dead Goat

Call it a dream.
Call it a field where you get lost
and no one goes out to find you.

Before the night
becomes too thick to breathe,
there are things you want
to remember.

But instead you taste
manzanilla, *estafiate*,
yerba buena, herbs
your grandmother sweetened with fire
to make you strong.
Remember

when you could raise
your kid above your head
with one hand?

Now you're a lame animal
whose entrails God will use
to see His unraveling.

He knows you are
where faith is all there is
and you have no use for it.

Everything else: lost in light.

Go Hungry

Go hungry every night
So the stars may blaze
Like oranges
In the moist sunlight

So the sky's mantle
May bring your mother's table
Overflowing
With her hands' work

Chicken soup and tortillas
With burnt edges

Leather belts and coat-hangers
Reminding you of bruises
one must give for love

And that voice, eternal voice
That spills to the floor like brick dust

Fine and unrelenting.

Message

Though you rest now
In a kingdom
God and worms

Know best

I could not go on
Without sending you a text
To tell you

That I'll make you up
As I made up stories
About the loves I never had

About the kisses
That never found a way
To leave my lips

All stories
All of them lies
All of them true

Like the evening that is
Its own light
Attracting with each passing minute

More of what I want
To keep for myself
And yet all of who I am

Keeps leaving me

Keeps packing suitcases
And writing emails
And sending texts

And leaving messages on Facebook
So I that I may remember
To return to the living

If I stray too far

Landlords

You're a stranger to them.
They've seen smoke zigzag
out of your lungs.
Have seen you smash a fly
with your favorite book.

When you're not in, they find
a crucifix smeared with lipstick,
sweep under the sofa
an eyelash made of bone.

Embarrassed, they open
your handbag and find
a bicycle on fire, a polished
cranium, two green cents.

Every day they see you descend,
have seen you soak with daylight
underneath your coat.
Every day they're relieved the gun
hasn't turned against you.

It takes its time.
They've seen how bad you want it.
They want you in love.

Ramona, Mostly Naked, Mostly Sane

Her nipples look like raisins.
Through a keyhole,

I see her.
I must be eight-years old.

I'm not a pervert.
But I see her.

Father Time brings
his Judas Cradle.

I smell her howls.
She calls a name.

I think it's Jesus.
Or Juan.

I spy on you, Ramona.
I sweep the broken skin

Of your wasted life.
Throw it at their feet.

Drawing Humans and Animals, Heads Represented by Circles, Bodies by Straight Lines

When I draw a stick figure,
it's always a woman, tiptoeing out
of the page, demanding
to be fed, sheltered, loved.

Sometimes it's my mother
who tries to cover the sound
of her footsteps with a white sheet.

She doesn't want to wake me,
knowing that if I go back to a place
before I was born,
I'll hold on to her like a thief
gripping his last breath.

Pobre Madre!

She doesn't see that she's fleshless,
and that her bone marrow is nothing more
than marks of lead
that can easily be erased
by my hand.

Other times it's my sister who comes
with both eyes empty of light.

Her hands are thin and cast
crow-like shadows on the wall.
She reaches out to me
sensing that I want to start over.
But she's the invisible thing leaning its weight
against the water,

a suicide no one wants to lower to the floor.

If you want to carry nothingness,
then carry it along with dog shit
in a brown paper bag, she still says.

I hear you *niña de mi alma!*
even if your tongue is sliced by paper.

Then there are times when my mother
and my sister have enough of me
and send the woman both of them disliked.

First I draw the contours of her labia
and find the clearing
the heat of her thighs
keeps moist.

I draw myself in the shape of a dog
and lick her cunt.

By then, I've slipped into her pulp
and I'm not in love
with the world,
nor with the only woman
who would love me,

a woman whose face is always in profile
whichever way it turns.

Fugitive

Your wife's sweet distances.
Where are they?
    Last night you slept next to her.
The sensual striptease
    of the moon gushed
through a sliver
        of open curtain.
At that hour,
    you wanted to be water
        drinking itself, not water
afraid of freezing.
In that quiet,
    a greater mind couldn't finish
the abandoned project
    you became.
You're driving now
    through another
Texas town,
        dust holding things in place
like a rib cage.
The light,
    hard as granite.

Birth

Speaking of the calf

born dead,

I have no opinion.

You have seen its legs

bent underneath its weight,

the half-open mouth,

and the moist fur

nightfall could not shape

into a thing for mourning.

It reminds you of the branch

whose drifting ceases

between two stones.

In my case, I can't say

I remember not being.

But if you must know,

it returns me to your waist

when the fog fastens

to the trees at night,

and I am taken by the quiet

pull of your body.

Heaven

I ask my son how
he pictures heaven
and he says that when he dies
he wants to go
to where there's no dust,
no nosebleeds,
no girls that'll make fun
of his haircut.
Your hair looks cool, I say,
and his nine year-old mouth
curls into a frown.
I understand how he feels,
the nine year-old boy I was
never left the barren playground
my adult life has become.
Years ago, I used to see him
as I drove home,
miles deep into drunk,
regretting at every swerve
the awful destination
I had set my life to.
He would sit next to me and wag
his finger, *no, no, no,*
and my *yes, yes, yes,*
would shut him down
like a building marked condemned.
Years later, I would see him
as I drove from town to town
intent on finding work
despite the heartlessness
the world poked into my chest
with its bullying finger.
The boy I was, was there,
striking a match taken
from my mother's kitchen

without her knowing,
threatening to burn
the cowardice I'd stored
like beetle-infested grain
in the silo of my body.
Maybe it's me all over again,
I think, as I watch this boy
slurp a milkshake.
I look hard into my son's eyes
to see if I can find
the dust I had damned to hell
when I was nine.

Sonnet with All Its Grief Cut Out

The mailbox of your life, always empty.
The woman you loved twenty years ago
Sleeps and breathes next to her plumber husband.
    Their kids, all grown up. The house is quiet,
Ready once again to be filled with moans.

    You listen, eyes closed, awake.
You suck on the nipples of the huge night.

Box of Pennies

For every penny I toss in here,
a man will lose a finger at his job.
A woman will get a broken nose at a bar for saying
some absurd thing that someone else mistook
as racist. It's a game.
The pennies in my pockets,
and this box that once kept light
from ruining photographs taken on days
happiness glazed our eyes with smiles.
A picnic.
The neighbor's divorce party.
But no one takes pictures at funerals,
sighed a man who'd missed
his best friend's burial.
It's a game of waiting,
this man, who once stole cars
for a living, knows.
It's waiting to hear music
we dreamed centuries before our birth,
waiting for our sleeplessness
to be defined as *rest*.
And then to think
that there's no greatness
more useless than to see
yourself in a picture:
fifteen years old,
an open smile that seeks, that yearns,
and chokes with the heat of a small flame.
Who's looking at whom?
There's a penny here for all the psalms
I've written on the dark skin of the years,
and a box that swears allegiance
to no song.

[All of us have a story]

All of us have a story
we want to tell, a story that loses
all courage once it reaches the tip
of our senses.
Afraid, like a man held at gunpoint,
it slips behind the mind's metal curtain.
No one can hear it,
and it can touch no one.
In its silence, it believes that history
has cut its tongue.
But it has a tongue, this story
that wants to erase itself,
disappear like a water stain
on a piece of paper.
Here's a story:
You want money.
You want children.
You want honesty.
I could be wrong.
Maybe all you want is never to get old
and find a clearing where the moon
can undress you.
Maybe it's all about getting lost
in the mesh of a big city
or in an unfamiliar desert
where the scorpions and the rats
leave you scribbles on the sand.
Maybe.
But who knows?
Maybe all you truly want is to have a story
and be able to say that your eyes
never found the star
you named as a child
to guide you.

If I Go Missing

I won't improvise desire.
If I do, I'll end up talking to some
stranger long dead, some murdered
young girl everyone felt sorry for.
A good thing for empathy.
All of us still fear the sharp edge
of uncertainty.
What if we're taken in the middle
of our daughter's ball game, or from our beds,
minutes after making love,
never to be seen again?
But who takes us?
Where do we go when someone in the news
says, *He's been missing for days.*
Few know.
Maybe the ones
who leave us by will or by some other way
not of their own choosing.
Maybe those who live
and choose not to return.
If you wake to find my toothbrush by the sink,
unused,
and my boots just right
underneath the bed
as I tend to leave them,
slip back under the covers and sleep
and dream new details—
a lit candle, a coffin, someone walking away—
in the shallow of my eyes.
Encounter once again so many
new images and words and trifles
that might or might not have been mine,
so new your life by then,
like newly discovered scenes
in a movie you hadn't seen in years.

Author Bio:
Octavio Quintanilla's poems have appeared in *Salamander, RHINO, Alaska Quarterly Review, The Bitter Oleander, Los Angeles Review, Border Crossing, Conium Review,* and elsewhere. His critical reviews have appeared in *Texas Books in Review* and in *Southwestern American Literature*.

www.ingramcontent.com/pod-product-compliance
Ingram Content Group UK Ltd.
Pitfield, Milton Keynes, MK11 3LW, UK
UKHW041948230426
12048UKWH00008B/215